Animal Activities

Animals Talking

JANE BURTON

Belitha Press

First published in Great Britain in 1990 by
Belitha Press Limited
31 Newington Green, London N16 9PU

Editor/Art Director: Treld Bicknell

Printed in the UK for Imago Publishing

British Library Cataloguing in Publication Data

Burton, Jane, *1933-*
Talking
1. Animals. Behaviour – For children
I. Title II. Series
591.51

ISBN 0 947553 87 8

Animals speak loudly and clearly, not only with their voices but with their whole bodies. They talk with ears and eyes and tails, and by standing up tall or crouching low, or even rolling over.

◀ This kitten needs help. He has climbed up a wall but dare not jump down again. He miaows plaintively and looks appealing.

A Red Fox vixen wants her cub to stay behind. She turns on him with ears flat, snarling. The cub understands, and goes back home. ▲

Male birds shout at the tops of their voices, each telling other males, 'This place belongs to *me!* Keep out!'

▲ This pair of Lesser Black-backed Gulls have got a nest on the ground. The male is calling with a raucous cry, advertising that this is *his* nest site.

The male Song Thrush sings among the apple branches. His voice is sweet and melodious, but his message to other thrushes is just the same. ▲

▲ Birds also call to their mates, and this Rook is cawing to his hen in the top of the tree.

These Starlings have nested in a special box put up for them on the side of a house. Only one nestling at a time can poke its head out of the hole to be fed. One parent has just stuffed a beakful of grubs down its throat but it still squawks for more. The adult churrs, not at the greedy baby, but to its mate who waits nearby, ready to fly off on another grub-collecting trip in the fields. ▲

◀ The bantam cock stands up tall, claps his wings and crows 'Cock-a-doodle-doo'! He is telling other cocks that *he* owns this patch.

▲ A hen talks quietly to her chicks – 'Plook-plook-plook' – and they cheep back. When she finds food, she calls them with an urgent food-call and they all run to get it.

Another hen protects her own chicks by spreading her wings and screeching a warning. She is telling the two strangers to go away! ▲

◀ Snorkel comes in from hunting and greets her kittens with a happy chirruping sound. They run to her, mewing contentedly, and rub around her while she licks them. They all purr with pleasure.

▲ When Fergus strolls by, Ginger goes to meet him, tail straight up in friendly greeting. But Fergus is *not* friendly and lashes out fast. Ginger ducks faster!

When Ginger is nearly grown up, he and Fergus caterwaul and spit whenever they meet. Ginger crouches with ears flat and curled tail, telling his father that he knows who's boss, and he's just leaving anyway. ▲

Dogs bark to guard their homes and scare away strangers, but they also talk in many other ways. They talk with their tails – 'up' means bossy and confident, droopy means unsure, and wagging says pleased. Jasper lets his puppies climb all over him, but now Boris keeps tugging at his ruff. Jasper growls a warning. Boris rolls over, showing his tummy, so Jasper won't snap at him.

Hans and Honey are friends and show that they like each other by wagging their tails and making friendly little noises whenever they meet.

Quince is only three weeks old. He crawls away from his brothers and sisters, then feels lonely and lost. He lifts up his muzzle and wails. Honey hears his dismal distress call and rushes to find him. Quince wags his tail and paws at her muzzle.

Lady digs a hole in the lawn while Emma watches. After much hard work they lie down beside the hole. Now Fan wants to dig, too. Fan and Lady bare their teeth and grizzle at each other. Emma looks a little nervous in case they snarl at her.

Bats use their voices to find their way about. They make high-pitched squeaks and listen to the sounds that bounce back. How long the echoes take to reach them, tells how far objects are away. This Serotine Bat has tracked a flying moth with ultrasonic squeaks, but when it talks to other bats, it chitters in a deeper voice. ▲

Bottle-nosed Dolphins navigate by beaming sounds, not from their mouths but through their foreheads. But when a dolphin talks to other dolphins, it makes noises through its blowhole. ▶

Moths can call to each other from a long way off by sending smell messages through the air. A newly-hatched female gives off a powerful scent. The male, like this ◀ African Emperor Moth, has huge feathery antennae for collecting the scent. As soon as he smells a female, he flies to her.

▲ A female Glow-worm waves her glowing abdomen in the dark to attract her mate.

This Honeybee has found new food. When she is full, she will fly back to the hive to tell the other workers, showing them how far to fly and in which direction by waggling her body in a special little dance. ▲

Male grasshoppers and crickets have songs and sing for the same reasons as birds: to warn other males away and to call their mates. The Bog Bush-cricket sings by rubbing his wings together. When the female hears him chirruping, she may respond – if he is lucky! – by crawling towards him.

This Stripe-winged Grasshopper sings by moving his legs up and down. Tiny pegs on his legs rub against his wings to make a wheezy song. Grasshoppers love the sun and sing best on hot days.

The sea is full of shrimps and crabs signalling to one another – some noisily and others with silent gestures.

▼ The Mantis Shrimp is a fearsome beast that can deliver a knock-out blow by aiming sound waves at a rival male. With its special folded front legs it makes a noise like a pistol shot!

When the tide goes out, the male Fiddler Crab comes out of his mud burrow to feed, daintily picking up bits with his one little claw. He signals by waving his other, huge, claw as if beckoning to females, but to male fiddlers he is saying, stay away from *my* patch of mud! ▼

◀ Frogs and toads do not say much except in spring, and then the noise they make can be deafening. Inflatable sacs of skin amplify their voices. Some blow out a small blister on each side of the head, but the African Common Toad pumps up one enormous balloon under his chin.

▲ Reptiles, too, are generally silent creatures, but most hiss in warning. The Adder is venomous, and other animals don't need to be warned to leave it alone.

This male Three-horned Chameleon puffs out his throat at the same time as he hisses at another male, telling him to go and find his own bush to sit in. ▲

Another warning that all animals understand is a sharp *thump!* The sound carries a long way and makes everyone look up to see what danger threatens. These Mongolian Gerbils are on the alert because one of them is drumming on the rock with his hind feet. They stand up tall, looking, listening, sniffing – ready to bolt to their burrows.

This Orange Rex rabbit has also heard a thump. He passes on the warning, stamping both hind feet on the ground. If nothing dangerous appears, he can relax and go on feeding.

Bassie, a tame African Grey Parrot, is a great 'talker'. When he is hungry, he says, 'Have a grape!' When the light is switched off at bedtime, he says, 'Goodnight Bassie!' Sometimes he says 'Goodnight' when the light is switched *on*. He associates the words with food or the light switch, but he doesn't understand what they really mean.

Charlie, a Yellow-fronted Amazon Parrot, says fewer words but mimics many sounds. She whistles, barks, pours water, laughs and sings.

Wild parrots talk to each other in parrot language. They shriek and squawk, bob their heads and dance and flap. We can mimic their calls, but we do not understand what they are saying, any more than they understand when they mimic our words.

Three ponies are putting their heads together over the fence and it looks as if they are gossiping. One pony has a new foal, and has not met the others since before he was born. She looks as if she is telling her friends what a naughty boy he is, and they are saying 'Tut tut, we know what colts are like'! Of course it is more likely they are just saying 'Hello' again by breathing up each other's nostrils and smelling each other's breath. This is the friendly way in which ponies greet one another.